"Lovespirations"

Reverend Ann Kathryn Bass-Lister

Copyright © 2022

by Reverend Ann Kathryn Bass-Lister

Editor: Jessica James, Rhema Consulting

ISBN#: 978-0-578-38692-8

TABLE OF CONTENTS

Take Care of Yourself First 7

Rising Above the Clouds 9

Imagine a Different World 12

What Does It Mean to Become Spiritually
Conscious?.......................................15

Unconscious.... Unresolved Anger 18

What Does It Mean to be Free? 21

Moving Through the Storm.....................23

Dealing with Fear 25

Gratitude 27

Letting Go 28

The Power of Prayer 30

Closing 33

A Note from the Teacher...........

"When you learn teach, when you get give."

-Maya Angelou

"Fierce – Femme"

The two words above, are written on the cover of my book to describe my persona as interpreted by Keshia Chapple, one of my Millennial Sisters. Fierce and Femme means that I am a woman of strength. I was pleasantly surprised upon receiving a call from Keshia who asked me for my address, because she wanted to bring me a gift. It was not Christmas, nor was it my birthday. When she arrived and presented me with this beautiful 16X20 canvas art piece, I was both shocked and grateful, especially when Keshia said, "Ms. Ann I created this piece while quarantined during the pandemic, and when it was completed, I said, this reminds me of Ms. Ann."

Wow, what an honor! When someone who has only known you for approximately one or two years is able to discern who you are, it is amazing. As a result, I was directed by Spirit and with permission from Keshia to use this gift as the cover for my Lovespirations Self-Care Devotional because it is an accurate description of what happens when we practice self-care.

Self-care is extremely important for our well-being. In order to be effective in our service to others, whether it is our family, friends or clients it is essential for us to take care of our mind, body and spirit. All three elements make up the "self." It is actually our Mind and Spirit that control our bodies. In 1995 I decided to begin my journey to wellness, by seeking the care that I needed to heal my mind and spirit from past trauma.

If you have not already done so, I trust that you will begin a regimen of self-care. It only takes 5-10 minutes to read a love-note, which will give you something on which to reflect during your day. I encourage you to make a commitment to do the "soul work" that is needed for your spiritual growth. Life is Meant to Be Good! And I have discovered that Life is GOOD, when we do the "soul work" that is necessary for us to heal and fall in love with ourselves.

This is a Love-Note from My Heart!!!

Rev. Ann K. Lister, M.Div.

The following Love-notes were written from my heart. They are ways of practicing self-care that changed my life. Remember, you are the most important person you have. Without you, there would be a void in the heart of the universe.

Take Care of Yourself First

When traveling by airplane, right before take-off, the flight attendant gives a safety demonstration. One of the most important aspects of the demonstration is how to use the oxygen mask: "If there is a reduction in air pressure, an oxygen mask will automatically appear in front of you. To start the flow of oxygen, pull the mask towards you. Place it firmly over your nose and mouth, secure the elastic band behind your head, and breathe normally. Although the bag does not inflate, oxygen is flowing to the mask. If you are traveling with a child or someone who requires assistance, secure your mask on first, and then assist the other person."

This is a metaphor for life. When there is a reduction in air pressure, (When someone in your life is sucking the air out of you) an oxygen mask will automatically appear in front of you. In life, this oxygen mask represents God's presence if we recognize it. To start the flow of oxygen, pull the mask towards you (Breathe into God's love, and allow God's oxygen to resuscitate your mind, body and spirit) then breathe normally. The flight attendant then says "If you are traveling with a child or someone who requires assistance, secure your mask on first, and then assist the other person." Before you can assist, and support the breathing and welfare of your partner, children, Mother, Father, sister, brother, your friend, you must put on YOUR mask first! WHY? Because you cannot help any of them if you have run out of oxygen".

Many of us are going through life, giving all of our oxygen away and wondering why we are always tired and have no energy. According to Dr. Bruce Lipton, when you give your energy away, especially in toxic spaces, you are creating stress and promoting the death of your healthy blood cells. If you don't take care of yourself first, you cannot take care of others. To take care of yourself is to own who you are and to love yourself fiercely, why? Because you are a beautiful emanation of God's Love!

Rising Above the Clouds

"Be Still and Know That I Am God"

Psalms: 46:10

There are so many metaphors for life when we are spiritually conscious. I invite and encourage you to pay attention to the random thoughts that enter your mind when you are sitting in silence—when you are still. I invite you to slow down and listen to life. It is always telling us something if we read between the lines. That is why the Psalmist said, "Be still, and know that I am God." It is in the stillness that we can get answers to any question we have about issues we are facing, and about our lives in general. In May, I took a flight to Atlanta, Georgia to attend my ten-year Spelman Class Reunion and as the plane taxied down the runway, and moved into take-off position, I looked outside the window, and said to myself, "Wow, it is really cloudy and gray." However, as we moved swiftly through the clouds reaching the cruising altitude of 30,000 feet, the sun began to break through the clouds, and before I knew it, the clouds had disappeared. The plane had moved through the darkness into the light.

It occurred to me during this moment of awareness that this is what happens in life. Sometimes, our lives are dark and cloudy which means that we find it difficult to come out of the dark place, but as we grow we are able to push through until we reach the light. Roman Catholic Carmelite, mystic and priest, St. John of the Cross wrote a poem about this experience called *The Dark Night of the Soul.* It was a metaphor for what it means when we cannot see our way through—it is a time when we find that our souls have gone down in a hole. Lead guitarist and founder of the group Alice in Chain, put it this way, *"Down in a hole, and I don't know if I can be saved; See my heart I decorate it like a grave; Oh, you don't understand who they thought I was supposed to be; Look at me now I'm a man (woman) who won't let himself/herself be."* This song is about a man who has lost his way, he is depressed like so many of us today. To use the analogy of the gray and cloudy day, this is a song about being in a dark and cloudy state of mind.

Many of our lives are filled with gray or dark clouds because we don't know how to rise above them. Therefore, we are in constant turmoil and we find ourselves, "down in a hole" and cannot see our way out. We see ourselves as victims because we don't feel loved, respected, or worthy of anything that we perceive as good. We are "down in a hole" because we have not dealt with childhood, teenage, or young adult trauma. According to the songwriter, we remain in the hole because we doubt whether we can be saved—our hearts are broken into pieces and we bury those pieces in the grave of our souls, which lead us deeper into the hole. We have no hope, and we keep slipping deeper and deeper into the hole. But my friend, there is hope and help.

You CAN rise above the clouds and move out of the darkness, but you must come face to face with your past. I hear you saying, "It is too painful!" I know it is painful, but you must rise out of your circumstances and into the sunlight. You can begin by talking with the God of creation who created you in the image of Divine Love. That is why Jesus the Christ was sent to earth because we needed someone in human form to show us the way to love and life. Jesus was sent to reach those of us who can't seem to find our way through life; those of us "down in a hole" who are having difficulty climbing out of the hole.

After you have a heart-to-heart talk with God, find a safe space to process your pain—find a good counselor, take one day at a time, develop a spiritual practice that works for you, and be patient with your progress. Be still and know that God is working everything out for your highest good. Overcoming darkness takes time and practice, it will not happen overnight. Because it requires changing your behavior and learning a new way to live. Joe Dispensa, author of *You are the Placebo*, says that knowledge is held in our minds, and experienced in our bodies. Therefore, whatever you have experienced in your life, is in your DNA; it is stored in your cells, and it cannot be released until you decide to do the work which will ultimately give you the courage to rise above the clouds.

Imagine a Different World

But the fruit of the Spirit is love, joy, peace, forbearance, kindness, goodness, faithfulness, gentleness and self-control. Against such things, there is no law.

Galatians 5:22-23 (NIV)

In 1971, John Lennon wrote a song entitled, "Imagine." Ironically, those times were no different than what we are experiencing today. People were crying out for equality and not just civil rights, but human rights. Today, I would like for you to meditate on the following lyrics and think about where we are today, and what you can do to manifest this world as imagined by our Brother John.

Imagine there's no heaven, It's easy if you try, No hell below us, Above us only sky; Imagine all the people Living for today....Aha..ah...Imagine there's no countries; It isn't hard to do; Nothing to kill or die for; And no religion, too; Imagine all the people; Living life in peace....You...You may say I'm a dreamer; But I'm not the only one; I hope someday you'll join us; And the world will be as one; Imagine no possessions; I wonder if you can; No need for greed or hunger; A brotherhood of man; Imagine all the people; Sharing all the world...You...You may say I'm a dreamer; But I'm not the only one; I hope someday you'll join us; And the world will live as One.

These words by John Lennon reveal a poignant reality that continues to plague our world. Just like God spoke through the authors of our biblical text, God spoke through Lennon in the silence of his heart...yes some would say that he was a "dreamer" but my friends, dreams come true. Harriet Tubman was a dreamer; Rev. Pauli Murray was a dreamer; William Lloyd Garrison was a dreamer; Audre Lorde was a dreamer; Cesar Chavez was a dreamer; Harriet Beecher Stowe was a dreamer; Joan Baez was a dreamer; Mahatma Gandhi was a dreamer; Major Griffin-Gracy was a dreamer; Rev. Dr. Martin Luther King Jr. was a dreamer; there were and still are many dreamers who envision a more benevolent world.

In the passage referenced above, which is included in the letter to the Galatian Church, Apostle Paul is very clear about the fruit of the Spirit which can only be manifested when one is intentionally living and following the teachings of Jesus the Christ. Jesus was not a Christian, he was born into Judaism, and sent by God to teach the Ancient Jews what it meant to follow the law of love and not the law of morality. It was the followers of Jesus who created the movement that would ultimately manifest into different sects of the religion we call Christianity. We are informed by the author in Acts 11:26 that, "The disciples were called Christians first at Antioch." However, during that time, as well as now, there are inconsistencies in how Christianity is practiced.

There are Carnal Christians and Spiritual Christians. Carnal Christianity is the practice of religious doctrine without spiritual transformation, while Spiritual Christianity is to follow and practice the teachings of Christ which causes one to be "transformed by the renewing of his or her life" (Romans 12:2).

I invite you today to emulate the vision of John Lennon by becoming a dreamer—a dreamer of a better world where there is equity for all people. And, as you dream about this world where we will live as ONE, think about what you will do to expand your heart for this to happen. Remember, we can only change the world, one person at a time.

What Does It Mean to Become Spiritually Conscious?

Then he said to them all: "Whoever wants to be my disciple must deny themselves and take up their cross daily and follow me.

Luke 9:23

It took me about ten years to reach the apex of spiritual maturity after I decided to render myself powerless over my life. Or, when I decided to "take up my cross daily and follow Jesus." For one to take up their cross means to die metaphorically to one's self. But it does not happen instantaneously. That is why Jesus says according to Luke's Gospel to "take up your cross daily." In this context, the Greek translation of the word daily means "without intermission" Therefore, it is a lifetime process, and this lifetime process produces transformative change.

When I reached the apex, I began to get compliments from my peers—"What happened to you?" "Did you lose weight?" The answer to the first question was what happened to me is that I am at peace. Why was I at peace? Because I decided to deal with all of the issues in my life that kept me from being a vessel through which the "light of God" could shine. Yes, I did lose weight. I lost about 50 pounds of toxic waste from my mind and spirit. The ingredients in this toxic waste were Inner Scars from Family Dynamics which included Emotional Abuse and Rejection; Colorism— "You sure are pretty to be so dark;" and Fear of NOT being accepted by others. These are just a few ingredients that were contained in the toxic waste expelled from my mind, body, and spirit. How did I do it? "By Any Means Necessary"— Counseling, Meditation, Studying the Teachings of Jesus, and the Letters of Apostle Paul. Why? Because I was sick and tired of living in mediocrity—because I wanted to be at peace with myself and others. Therefore, I had to do the work. I had to "take up my cross," and follow the teachings of Jesus not just on Sunday, but every day of the week. It became my way of life.

We were not born to live in mediocrity. We were born to grow, live up to our fullest potential, and make a difference in the world. Can you imagine what would happen if everyone born on the planet, did absolutely nothing—they did not grow emotionally, or physically, they did not discover new realities, they stayed in a little box, in a little town, where everyone did nothing. Of course, you can't imagine it, because life would not be worth living in that kind of world. It would be boring and non-productive. So, my sister and brother, why are you living in mediocrity? Why are you lowering your standards and accepting relationships that are not conducive to love and peace?

We are made in God's image, which means that the spirit of God is one with our spirit. We are Emanations of God's Perfect Love and Jesus is an example of God's perfect love. Love is the answer to all of life's problems. But we cannot love if we don't love ourselves first. When Jesus was questioned about the commandments by the religious establishment of his time, in Matthew 22:37, He responded: "Love the Lord your God with all your heart and with all your soul and with all your mind.' This is the first and greatest commandment. And the second is like it: `Love your neighbor as yourself.' If this is the greatest commandment, then this should be the foundation of our lives.

We may think that we are loving ourselves and others, but if there are conditions attached to the feelings that we call love, it is NOT love. If you are ready to stop living a life of mediocrity, choose LOVE—a JUST LOVE—a LOVE...that will set you FREE. BUT! You have got to do the work.

Unconscious....Unresolved Anger

What causes fights and quarrels among you? Don't they come from your desires that battle within you? You desire but do not have, so you kill. You covet but you cannot get what you want, so you quarrel and fight. You do not have because you do not ask God.

James 4:1-2New International Version (NIV)

Do you have unresolved anger? Before you answer, I want to preference this question with an explanation. I am not asserting that we should not get angry. Anger is a normal feeling. If we don't process the anger, however, it will fester, turn into rage, and manifest into dis-ease. We also become victims, blaming other people for our anger. This is pervasive in homes where there is domestic violence. The running narrative for most abusers is "She made me mad;" "He made me mad;" "You made me do it"—which is a way of not being accountable for their behavior. No one has the power to make anyone do anything. It is impossible for someone to go inside of another person's brain, and turn on an "angry" button. We are in control of our own minds, bodies and spirits.

Granted, the reason for some of our anger is legitimate but is not healthy if unresolved. Some of us are holding onto childhood anger because of something our parents said, did, or did not do; Some of us are holding on to incidents that occurred during elementary school, middle school, high school, college, or graduate school. Some of us were betrayed by a friend, lover or spouse, and we cannot let it go. The list can go on and on, because life is complex. The complexity centers around the fact that many of us don't know that we have unresolved anger, and we are unconsciously spreading toxic energy all over the place. In some cases, people can feel the negative energy emitting from our "being" when we walk into a room.

How do we know that we have unresolved anger? When we are driving, and someone cuts us off, do we feel the need to curse them out or throw them the finger, and not a friendly finger, you know the one. When we order food at a restaurant, and the waitress gets our order wrong, do we feel the need to yell at her? When our children are being children, and we walk into their bedroom, and the wall is filled with beautiful designs, from a black marker, do we start screaming at them? When our partner, spouse or otherwise, does not notice a new outfit, haircut or hairdo, or God forbid forget our birthday, anniversary, a date that is scheduled, or anything else, do we go into a rage?

Anger is often unconscious. We are not aware that it is there, even when someone points it out; because we have buried it so deep that we are unable to recognize that it still lives and is affecting our behavior. Author, and Spiritual Leader, Iyanla Vanzant, says, "Feelings buried alive never die." And, I have found that to be true.

I am writing this from my own experience. I am a survivor of domestic violence from a former marriage, and before I began my spiritual healing through counseling, and meditation, I was a victim. I had a pity party with life until I became aware of the underlying issues that were controlling my life. I internalized my anger, which manifested in passive-aggressive behavior; I was a people pleaser because I thought I could control other people's anger. "When we are victims we are not in reality, we only have perceptions of our reality" (unknown author). Thank God, I woke up over 20 years ago and began my work. If this resonates with you, I encourage you to consider seeking a safe space to process your anger. When healing takes place, your whole life will be transformed. In the words of Spiritual Leader, Rev. Dr. Michael Bernard Beckwith, "Change does not mean you are transformed, but transformation means you have gone through changes." If we find the courage to go through changes, one person at a time, the world will change. Because WE ARE THE WORLD.

What Does It Mean to be Free?

So if the Son (Christ) sets you free, you will be free indeed.

John 8:36 (NIV)

Freedom...what does it really mean to be free. If we look at the life of Viktor E. Frankl, who spent years in a Nazi death camp, we will discover that freedom is indeed a state of mind. In his book *Man's Search For Meaning,* Frankl stated, "In spite of all the enforced physical and mental primitiveness of the life in a concentration camp, it was possible for spiritual life to deepen." Sensitive people who were used to a rich intellectual life may have suffered much pain, but the damage to their inner selves was less. They were able to retreat from their terrible surroundings to a life of inner riches and spiritual freedom." I was inspired by this story because it is like the plight of my people who were enslaved, dehumanized, and stripped of their cultural reality, yet many of them survived, because of their "inner riches and spiritual freedom."

Although their bodies had been captured, their minds could remain free—free to soar to heights unknown. Free to soar into the heavens and talk to the ancestors who were with them—the ancestors who guided their minds to the Promised Land of peace. This same freedom is ours today. But we must look within to find it. We must come face to face with the reality that there is no separation between us and God. This is why Jesus was sent as God's Son or Spiritual Guide to show us the way to freedom. It is this freedom that enables us to love justly.

Moving Through the Storm

And there arose a great storm of wind, and the waves beat into the ship so that it was now full. And he was in the hinder part of the ship, asleep on a pillow; and they awake him, and say unto him, Master, carest thou not that we perish? And he arose, and rebuked the wind, and said unto the sea, Peace, be still. And the wind ceased, and there was a great calm.

Mark 4:37-39 (KJV)

Today, as I sat at my kitchen table, a storm blew in. We live in an apartment complex that is sectioned off by courtyards, so there are lots of trees and shrubbery. That is how I determined how hard the wind was blowing. I would imagine that it was consistent with the wind witnessed by Jesus' disciples on the boat. I also imagined what it would have felt and been like if I had been on an airplane. I believe that experiencing this storm on an airplane, probably would have felt like it did on a boat in the midst of turbulent water. It's SCARY FOLKS! In fact, I have silently whispered, "Peace Be Still," during turbulent times when traveling by airplane.

This, my sisters and brothers is consistent with the metaphorical storms that we experience in life. There are times when we experience rain, I call that the nudging.   There are times when we experience mild thunderstorms, this means that the challenges of life get a little more difficult, then we experience severe thunderstorms, which at this point, life is almost screaming. When tornados or hurricanes began to manifest, life has become destructive and falls apart. This, for many of us is the day of reckoning. It is the time when we are forced to decide to make changes in our lives.

There is help. Because when we go through the metaphorical storms of life, God is in the midst of the storm. If we listen carefully, we will discover that God is trying to tell us something. But, to hear what God is saying, we must be in tune with God's spirit. If we are not tuned in, the waves will overtake our boat. My sisters and my brothers, I encourage you to recognize what is going on when metaphorical storms come into your life. Storms come to teach. And, if we are open, God will show us what we need to learn in the storm, and we will not only grow, but eventually will have the strength to endure the storm no matter how strong. But, if our minds are closed and we choose to become a victim of the storm, we become vulnerable to anger and bitterness. Life is always teaching us, and storms are a part of the process.

Dealing with Fear

For God has not given us a spirit of fear, but of power and of love and of a sound mind.

2 Timothy, I:7 (NKJV)

Self-realization is also a form of self-care. It means to pay attention to our inner self, to understand that we are co-creators of our lives. That is why I want to bring awareness to fear and how it affects our lives. First, according to many experts on this subject, there is a healthy fear and an unhealthy fear. Healthy fear is the fear that we have when danger is nearby. It is a fear that causes us to either seek cover or run for our lives.

Unhealthy fear, for many of us, was taught by either verbal or non-verbal communication as children. As a result, many of us are still holding on to those fears. Many of us are in adult bodies but have not been able to reconcile with our little girl and boy fears. We have been limping through life allowing our fears to control our behavior. For some of us, it began in our home churches. As children, many of us were taught by our parents and the church, to be afraid of God. We were taught that God was a punitive, angry, and jealous God. We were also taught that we would go to "hell" if we were "bad." This was not only unhealthy, but it left "internal bruises" in the souls of many of us. Unlike external bruises which are on the surface of the skin, internal bruises lie dormant in our souls until triggered.

When our "internal bruises" are triggered, fear is activated and we either act out or shut down. Somewhere I heard a speaker give the following meaning for FEAR. It is False Evidence Appearing Real. This means that many times, our perception of what someone is feeling about us is just that; a perception. There are times when our fear is so overwhelming that it causes us to drive people who love us out of our lives. We drive them away because no matter how much that person assures us of their love, fear handicaps our ability to believe them. But, my sisters and brothers, President Franklin D. Roosevelt said, "There is nothing to fear, but fear itself." Why? Because fear, is only a perception, but it is dangerous when it is unchecked.

This Lovenote is not about blaming the church or anyone for the fear that is being experienced. It is about acknowledging that the fear is real and about setting yourself free by doing the work to overcome the fear. Most importantly, don't think that this process will happen overnight. It is a lifetime process and takes practice. I know, because I am over 25-years under construction. May God bless you as you enter the Fearless Zone, where you will be challenged, but rewarded.

Gratitude

Give thanks to the LORD, for he is good; his love

endures forever.

Psalm 107:1 (NIV)

When the sun rose this morning and peered through your window, what were you doing? Were you waking up from a deep sleep? Perhaps you were getting dressed for work or eating your breakfast. No matter what you were doing, if you did not pause in gratitude, I invite you to make this a part of your daily ritual. It only takes a few minutes. Why are you pausing in gratitude? You are pausing to give thanks to God for the opportunity to see another day; You are pausing to affirm and envision a safe and peaceful day for you and your family; You are pausing to give reverence to the God of the Universe who sustains you when you cannot sustain yourself. The attitude of gratitude and thankfulness will always return to us in the form of a blessing.

Letting Go

Do not judge, and you will not be judged. Do not condemn, and you will not be condemned. Forgive, and you will be forgiven.

Luke 6:37 (NIV)

In the preceding Gospel of Luke, Jesus is waxing eloquently with spiritual wisdom. I will focus on the last sentence which is "Forgive, and you will be forgiven." Life is reciprocal. What we want, we must give. There are several different meanings for the word "forgive" in Greek, however, I will use the verb that means "to let go."

Living life in the present means letting go of the past. This does not mean forgetting what you experienced; it means that you are no longer allowing it to control your life. I know how difficult it is to forgive someone that has betrayed you. I know how difficult it is to forgive someone who has spiritually, physically and mentally abused you. I also know how difficult it is to please some of our family members. Whether you have been betrayed, or abused, **Pain is Pain.** However, there comes a time when you must let it go if you want to live a quality life.

Many of us are stuck in this cycle of pain and unforgiveness for whatever reason and some of us are holding on to it for dear life. Do you want to stay stuck? Or do you want to be free to live the kind of life you were created to live? Do you realize how much the planet needs your gifts, and talents? That is why it is so vital for you to let the internal baggage go.

You have the power to let it go, but you must be willing. How? By making a conscious effort to practice letting go. It does not happen overnight, but with determination, it will happen. It will happen when you decide that you are tired of being angry, unhappy, depressed, resentful, and just downright miserable. It will happen when you acknowledge that you are a human being who was created and crafted in perfection. Not that you behave in a perfect manner, but that every cell in your body was made in the image of the creator who placed you on the planet to serve a purpose.

Letting go is a surrendering process that happens in stages. It requires that you find someone safe with whom you can release or process your feelings; develop a consistent meditation practice, even if it is only 10 minutes or less a day; write it down— "I forgive (whoever) for (whatever); affirm it daily, and watch God work. The change is subtle, but as you continue this process, one day it will occur to you that you are no longer reacting negatively when someone brings up the situation or person's name. This is self-care you are taking care of the spirit that resides deep inside of your soul. Most importantly, you are worth it!!! Because you are a Beautiful Emanation of God's Creation.

The Power of Prayer

Therefore, I tell you, whatever you ask for in prayer, believe that you have received it, and it will be yours.

Mark 11:24

And when you pray, do not be like the hypocrites, for they love to pray standing in the synagogues and on the street corners to be seen by others. Truly I tell you, they have received their reward in full. But when you pray, go into your room, close the door and pray to your Father, who is unseen. Then your Father, who sees what is done in secret, will reward you. And when you pray, do not keep on babbling like pagans, for they think they will be heard because of their many words. [8] Do not be like them, for your Father knows what you need before you ask him.

Matthew in 6:5-8

This is one of the most important aspects of self-care. I must be transparent about how prayer shaped my life when I learned to pray with intention. It came at a point in my life when I was, "sick and tired of being sick and tired of my empty life." On that day in November 1995, I got down on my knees and had a sincere conversation with the God of my understanding. It was the God that my

Grandmother, Katherine told me to trust. She said, "Just trust him Baby and he will make a way." She was right! I trusted God to transform my life.

This prayer proved to be my lesson on what it means to "surrender" because it was through this process that I learned the truth about intentional prayer. It is a reality that God knows what we need before we ask. I discovered that God knew exactly what I needed. I realized that when I prayed, I "woke up" all the places in my life that needed healing. In hindsight, I remember hearing people say that when they "gave their life to Christ the devil got busy." What I discovered, however was that my decision to surrender gave the Infinite Universal Wisdom or God, permission to begin "Open Heart Surgery" on me. How did that look? It was literally surgery with no anesthesia, because all of my issues began to come up, one at a time. It was as if I activated a "healing rod." I remember sharing what I was going through with one of my elders. And, he said, "God is working." I had no idea what he was talking about, but I do now. Because I discovered that all of the issues that came up in my life, were happening FOR me and not TO me.

The reason they were happening for me was because humans were created to not only grow physically, but spiritually. We were not created to remain stagnate. Therefore, intentional prayer is the key to eternal life and all of its riches. But, if we pray in the spirit of doubt and worry, we will continue to get more of that. I have heard some say "If you are going to pray, don't worry. If you are going to worry don't pray." In other words, why pray if you are going to worry about the outcome.

CLOSING

I trust that you have been blessed by the love-notes. I am dedicated to the healing of the whole person—spirit, mind and body. I am called by God-Divine Wisdom-Infinite Spirit to teach principles of new thinking for healing hearts and transforming lives as demonstrated by Jesus the Christ. The greatest commandment in the sacred text is to love unconditionally. However, I realized over 25 years ago that for me to follow that commandment, I must first love myself. I encourage you, if you have not begun this process to take the first step. Love is a vibrational energy that emits, peace, kindness, and patience. It is also nondiscriminatory. I encourage you to do the work, so that you may find the gift of love.

Reverend Ann Kathryn Bass-Lister, M.Div.

Clinically Trained Professional Chaplain, Speaker and Writer specializing in spiritual development, weddings, funerals and End of Life Care. Please feel free to email me at rev.ron.ann.lister@gmail.com with any questions

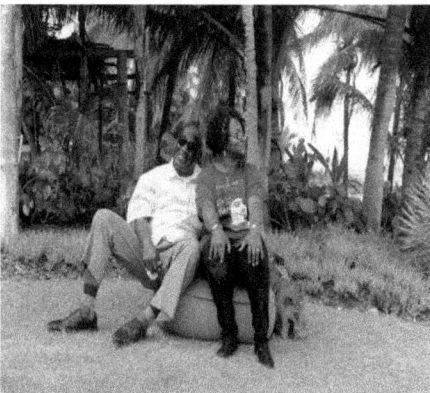

Rev. Ron & Rev. Ann Lister

www.ingramcontent.com/pod-product-compliance
Lightning Source LLC
Chambersburg PA
CBHW071950100426
42736CB00042B/2700